Greek Word of the Day:

365 High Frequency Words to Accelerate Your Greek Vocabulary

ISBN: 1530844304
ISBN–13: 978-1530844302

CONTENTS

INTRODUCTION

Learning a new language involves learning a lot of new vocabulary. Although the grammar and pronunciation of a language can seem like the most difficult parts, especially a difficult language like Greek, the real challenge quickly becomes learning the thousands of new words you require to speak a new language fluently.

How to find the right words and how to efficiently memorize them are the problems that many language learners face near the beginning of their studies. The goal of this book is to fill the gap by providing you with a new, high frequency Greek word to learn every day. At the end of the year (or much sooner) you will be 365 words closer to your goal of speaking Greek.

Did you know that in English, the most common 100 words make up nearly half of every sentence, and that other languages have similar frequency distributions? This is a powerful concept that is underused in many language courses. By focusing on the high frequency words, this book will accelerate your Greek vocabulary more efficiently than merely learning the random lists of words that learners sometimes face, and by providing the words to you, this book will save you from the time-consuming process of searching for all those new words yourself.

The outline of this book is a new word every day for a year. In this way you can be sure that you are making progress even on days where you don't have time to study. Carry this word around with you and review it throughout the day. Of course many people will progress faster through this book and will want more than one word a day and in that case the reader should go at whatever pace feels comfortable. I would still encourage you go back to the word of the day to review on that specific day, just to ensure that you have thoroughly learned it. Remember repetition is the mother of all learning.

Good luck on your language learning journey and I hope you enjoy your Greek Word of the Day!

THE GREEK ALPHABET
ΕΛΛΗΝΙΚΌ ΑΛΦΆΒΗΤΟ

The Modern Greek alphabet contains 24 letters and is written from left to right. The same basic Greek alphabet that is used today has been used to write Greek since the 8th century B.C.E.

Below is the complete Greek alphabet with a simple pronunciation guide for each letter. In Greek some letter combinations represent different sounds than you might expect, but a pronunciation guide is included in this book after each word to help you.

Uppercase	Lowercase	Pronunciation
A	α	a as in "father"
B	β	v as in "very"
Γ	γ	g as in "good", but deeper and throatier y as in "yes" before an "e" or "i" sound
Δ	δ	th as in "that", written dh
E	ε	e as in "dress" or ay as in "play" at the end of a word
Z	ζ	z as in "zoo"
H	η	ee as in "bee", written i
Θ	θ	th as in "think"
I	ι	ee as in "bee", written i
K	κ	k as in "kick"

Λ	λ	l as in "large"
M	μ	m as in "me"
N	ν	n as in "no"
Ξ	ξ	ks as in "kicks"
O	o	o as in "rope"
Π	π	p as in "pie"
P	ρ	rolled r as in the Spanish "rapido"
Σ	σ / ς	s as in "see"
T	τ	t as in "toe"
Y	υ	ee as in "bee", written i
Φ	φ	f as in "far"
X	X	ch as in Scottish "loch" or German "doch", written kh
Ψ	ψ	ps as in "sips"
Ω	ω	o as in "rope"

Modern Greek is not too hard to pronounce as an English speaker, but there are still some difficulties and I recommend going to forvo.com and typing in the words in this book to hear how a Greek native speaker would pronounce them.

Jan. 1

γέφυρα

[yéfira] (feminine)

bridge

Jan. 2

αλάτι

[aláti] (neuter)

salt

Jan. 3

χειμώνας

[khimónas] (masculine)

winter

Jan. 4

φτηνός

[ftinós]

cheap

Jan. 5

ψάρι

[psári] (neuter)

fish

Jan. 6

φρούτο

[frúto] (neuter)

fruit

Jan. 7

μουσείο

[musío] (neuter)

museum

Jan. 8

ωραίος

[oréos]

beautiful

Jan. 9

εγκέφαλος

[enkéfalos] (masculine)

brain

Jan. 10

χώρα

[khóra] (feminine)

country

Jan. 11

άσχημος

[áskhimos]

ugly

Jan. 12

θέλω

[thélo]

to want

Jan. 13

μωρό

[moró] (neuter)

baby

Jan. 14

πιπέρι

[pipéri] (neuter)

pepper (spice)

Jan. 15

διαμέρισμα

[dhiamérisma] (neuter)

apartment

Jan. 16

κορίτσι

[korítsi] (neuter)

girl

Jan. 17

πολεμώ

[polemó]

to fight

Jan. 18

ρίχνω

[ríkhno]

to throw

Jan. 19

υγρός

[igrós]

wet

Jan. 20

πράσινος

[prásinos]

green

Jan. 21

ειρήνη

[iríni] (feminine)

peace

Jan. 22

λεπτός

[leptós]

thin

Jan. 23

παντελόνι

[pantelóni] (neuter)

pants

Jan. 24

διαβάζω

[dhiavázo]

to read

Jan. 25

τίποτε

[típote]

nothing

Jan. 26

φύλλο

[fílo] (neuter)

leaf

Jan. 27

γελώ

[yeló]

to laugh

Jan. 28

ζεστός

[zestós]

hot

Jan. 29

στέκομαι

[stékome]

to stand

Jan. 30

κρεβατοκάμαρα

[krevatokámara] (feminine)

bedroom

Jan. 31

πόδι

[pódhi] (neuter)

leg

Feb. 1

ζωντανός

[zontanós]

alive

Feb. 2

γάμος

[gámos] (masculine)

wedding

Feb. 3

λαχανικό

[lakhanikó] (neuter)

vegetable

Feb. 4

μισό

[misó] (neuter)

half

Feb. 5

σώμα

[sóma] (neuter)

body

Feb. 6

καρχαρίας

[karkharías] (masculine)

shark

Feb. 7

λίγο

[lígo]

a little

Feb. 8

χαμογελώ

[khamoyeló]

to smile

Feb. 9

αβγό

[avgó] (neuter)

egg

Feb. 10

κάποιος

[kápios]

somebody

Feb. 11

ιδέα

[idhéa] (feminine)

idea

Feb. 12

μαύρος

[mávros]

black

Feb. 13

σαγόνι

[sagóni] (neuter)

chin

Feb. 14

στεγνός

[stegnós] (masculine)

dry

Feb. 15

βορράς

[vorás] (masculine)

north

Feb. 16

πηδώ

[pidhó]

to jump

Feb. 17

μακρύς

[makrís]

long

Feb. 18

αυτί

[aftí] (neuter)

ear

Feb. 19

άνοιξη

[ániksi] (feminine)

spring (season)

Feb. 20

χείλος

[khílos] (neuter)

lip

Feb. 21

δωμάτιο

[dhomátio] (neuter)

room

Feb. 22

λυπημένος

[lipiménos]

sad

Feb. 23

πρόβλημα

[próvlima] (neuter)

problem

Feb. 24

σύζυγος

[sízigos] (masculine or feminine)

spouse (husband or wife)

Feb. 25

κάτι

[káti] (neuter)

something

Feb. 26

πλάτη

[pláti] (feminine)

back (body)

Feb. 27

πρωινό

[proinó] (neuter)

breakfast

Feb. 28

τώρα

[tóra]

now

Feb. 29

Παναγιώτης

[Pana:otis]

Panagiotis

Mar. 1

τί

[ti]

what

Mar. 2

πέφτω

[péfto]

to fall

Mar. 3

αεροδρόμιο

[aerodhrómio] (neuter)

airport

Mar. 4

καφές

[kafés] (masculine)

coffee

Mar. 5

πρόσωπο

[prósopo] (neuter)

face

Mar. 6

πάρκο

[párko] (neuter)

park

Mar. 7

εργασία

[ergasía] (feminine)

job

Mar. 8

βοηθώ

[voithó]

to help

Mar. 9

θάλασσα

[thálasa] (feminine)

sea

Mar. 10

καλοκαίρι

[kalokéri] (neuter)

summer

Mar. 11

δύσκολος

[dhískolos]

difficult

Mar. 12

άνεμος

[ánemos] (masculine)

wind

Mar. 13

πίνω

[píno]

to drink

Mar. 14

μπίρα

[bíra] (feminine)

beer

Mar. 15

ξυπνώ

[ksipnó]

to wake up

Mar. 16

στυλό

[stiló] (neuter)

pen

Mar. 17

χυμός

[khimós] (masculine)

juice

Mar. 18

πορτοκαλί

[portokalí]

orange (color)

Mar. 19

αγοράζω

[agorázo]

to buy

Mar. 20

κοντός

[kontós]

short

Mar. 21

διάσημος

[dhiásimos]

famous

Mar. 22

λαιμός

[lemós] (masculine)

neck

Mar. 23

πετώ

[petó]

to fly

Mar. 24

φούστα

[fústa] (feminine)

skirt

Mar. 25

σαλάτα

[saláta] (feminine)

salad

Mar. 26

κοτόπουλο

[kotópulo] (neuter)

chicken

Mar. 27

πεθαίνω

[pethéno]

to die

Mar. 28

πόλεμος

[pólemos] (masculine)

war

Mar. 29

πόρτα

[porta] (feminine)

door

Mar. 30

μπλε

[ble]

blue

Mar. 31

κατασκευάζω

[kataskevázo]

to make

Apr. 1

χοιρινό

[khirinó] (neuter)

pork

Apr. 2

νότος

[nótos] (masculine)

south

Apr. 3

λίθος

[líthos] (masculine)

stone

Apr. 4

πρώιμος

[próimos]

early

Apr. 5

ιατρός

[iatrós] (masculine)

doctor

Apr. 6

εβδομάδα

[evdhomádha] (feminine)

week

Apr. 7

αργά

[argá]

late

Apr. 8

καρδιά

[kardhiá] (feminine)

heart

Apr. 9

ομπρέλα

[ombréla] (feminine)

umbrella

Apr. 10

πάντα

[pánda]

always

Apr. 11

ακολουθώ

[akoluthó]

to follow

Apr. 12

περπατώ

[perpató]

to walk

Apr. 13

ντομάτα

[domáta] (feminine)

tomato

Apr. 14

συνάντηση

[sinántisi] (feminine)

meeting

Apr. 15

κάμερα

[kámera] (feminine)

camera

Apr. 16

βλέπω

[vlépo]

to see

Apr. 17

νερό

[neró] (neuter)

water

Apr. 18

λύκος

[líkos] (masculine)

wolf

Apr. 19

κουζίνα

[kuzína] (feminine)

kitchen

Apr. 20

πλένω

[pléno]

to wash

Apr. 21

όνομα

[ónoma] (neuter)

name

Apr. 22

δάσος

[dhásos] (neuter)

forest

Apr. 23

ψεύδομαι

[psévdhome]

to tell a lie

Apr. 24

κόρη

[kóri] (feminine)

daughter

Apr. 25

ρούχο

[rúkho] (neuter)

clothing

Apr. 26

χορτάρι

[khortári] (neuter)

grass

Apr. 27

στόμα

[stóma] (neuter)

mouth

Apr. 28

αστυνομία

[astinomía] (feminine)

police

Apr. 29

πιάνω

[piáno]

to catch

Apr. 30

οικογένεια

[ikoyénia] (feminine)

family

May 1

νικώ

[nikó]

to win

May 2

χιόνι

[khióni] (neuter)

snow

May 3

μητέρα

[mitéra] (feminine)

mother

May 4

αστέρι

[astéri] (neuter)

star

May 5

ξέρω

[kséro]

to know

May 6

άλογο

[álogo] (neuter)

horse

May 7

γουρούνι

[gurúni] (neuter)

pig

May 8

λίμνη

[límni] (feminine)

lake

May 9

τραβώ

[travó]

to pull

May 10

αρνί

[arní] (neuter)

lamb

May 11

μπότα

[bóta] (feminine)

boot

May 12

γράφω

[gráfo]

to write

May 13

μεγαλώνω

[megalóno]

to grow

May 14

ουρανός

[uranós] (masculine)

sky

May 15

χοιρομέρι

[khiroméri] (neuter)

ham

May 16

άνθρωπος

[ánthropos] (masculine)

human

May 17

κρασί

[krasí] (neuter)

wine

May 18

γλώσσα

[glósa] (feminine)

language, tongue

May 19

νησί

[nisí] (neuter)

island

May 20

παππούς

[papús] (masculine)

grandfather

May 21

βουνό

[vunó] (neuter)

mountain

May 22

ποτάμι

[potámi] (neuter)

river

May 23

εστιατόριο

[estiatório] (neuter)

restaurant

May 24

σταφύλι

[stafíli] (neuter)

grape

May 25

σκύλος

[skílos] (masculine)

dog

May 26

παίζω

[pézo]

to play

May 27

πατέρας

[patéras] (masculine)

father

May 28

ανοίγω

[anígo]

to open

May 29

σχολείο

[skholío]

school

May 30

ελπίζω

[elpízo]

to hope

May 31

ίδιος

[ídhios]

same

Jun. 1

τούρτα

[túrta] (feminine)

cake

Jun. 2

λεπτό

[leptó] (neuter)

minute

Jun. 3

τηλεόραση

[tileórasi] (feminine)

television

Jun. 4

ανατολή

[anatolí] (feminine)

east

Jun. 5

κρεβάτι

[kreváti] (neuter)

bed

Jun. 6

τελειώνω

[telióno]

to end

Jun. 7

πουλώ

[puló]

to sell

Jun. 8

αγρόκτημα

[agróktima] (neuter)

farm

Jun. 9

πολιτισμός

[politismós]

culture

Jun. 10

τοίχος

[tíkhos] (masculine)

wall

Jun. 11

ήρεμος

[íremos]

quiet

Jun. 12

ανεβαίνω

[anevéno]

to climb

Jun. 13

οδηγώ

[odhigó]

to drive

Jun. 14

αεροπλάνο

[aeropláno] (neuter)

airplane

Jun. 15

μέλλον

[mélon] (neuter)

future

Jun. 16

ποντίκι

[pontíki] (neuter)

mouse

Jun. 17

αδύναμος

[adhínamos]

weak

Jun. 18

χτίζω

[khtízo]

to build

Jun. 19

ξενοδοχείο

[ksenodhokhío] (neuter)

hotel

Jun. 20

σταθμός

[stathmós] (masculine)

station (train)

Jun. 21

σήμερα

[símera]

today

Jun. 22

χορτοφάγος

[khortofágos]

vegetarian

Jun. 23

ακριβός

[akrivós]

expensive

Jun. 24

σκέφτομαι

[skéftome]

to think

Jun. 25

νοσοκομείο

[nosokomío] (neuter)

hospital

Jun. 26

πορτοκάλι

[portokáli] (neuter)

orange (fruit)

Jun. 27

αστράγαλος

[astrágalos] (masculine)

ankle

Jun. 28

γάλα

[gála] (neuter)

milk

Jun. 29

παπούτσι

[papútsi] (neuter)

shoe

Jun. 30

τρέχω

[trékho]

to run

Jul. 1

επιχείρηση

[epikhírisi] (feminine)

business

Jul. 2

άρρωστος

[árostos]

sick

Jul. 3

μύτη

[míti] (feminine)

nose

Jul. 4

κόβω

[kóvo]

to cut

Jul. 5

βοδινό

[vodhinó] (neuter)

beef

Jul. 6

όπλο

[óplo] (neuter)

weapon

Jul. 7

ήλιος

[ílios] (masculine)

sun

Jul. 8

μιλώ

[miló]

to speak

Jul. 9

πάγος

[págos] (masculine)

ice

Jul. 10

πλούσιος

[plúsios]

rich

Jul. 11

πότε

[póte]

when

Jul. 12

μπαρ

[bar] (neuter)

bar (place to drink)

Jul. 13

τουαλέτα

[tualéta] (feminine)

bathroom

Jul. 14

πληρώνω

[piróno]

to pay

Jul. 15

αδελφός

[adhelfós] (masculine)

brother

Jul. 16

ποιος

[pios]

who

Jul. 17

δικηγόρος

[dhikigóros] (masculine)

lawyer

Jul. 18

πολλοί

[polí]

many

Jul. 19

χρόνος

[khrónos] (masculine)

year

Jul. 20

περιβόλι

[perivóli] (neuter)

garden

Jul. 21

τρώγω

[trógo]

to eat

Jul. 22

λεωφορείο

[leoforío] (neuter)

bus

Jul. 23

πουλί

[pulí] (neuter)

bird

Jul. 24

χαρτί

[khartí] (neuter)

paper

Jul. 25

γένι

[yéni] (neuter)

beard

Jul. 26

αίμα

[éma] (neuter)

blood

Jul. 27

μέταλλο

[métalo] (neuter)

metal

Jul. 28

νύχτα

[níkhta] (feminine)

night

Jul. 29

σούπα

[súpa] (feminine)

soup

Jul. 30

χορεύω

[khorévo]

to dance

Jul. 31

χωριό

[khorió] (neuter)

village

Aug. 1

οδός

[odhós] (feminine)

street

Aug. 2

πλαστικό

[plastikó] (neuter)

plastic

Aug. 3

φάρμακο

[fármako] (neuter)

medicine

Aug. 4

μολύβι

[molívi] (neuter)

pencil

Aug. 5

ήδη

[ídhi]

already

Aug. 6

πιάτο

[piáto] (neuter)

plate

Aug. 7

νεκρός

[nekrós]

dead

Aug. 8

εισιτήριο

[isitírio] (neuter)

ticket

Aug. 9

δύση

[dhísi] (feminine)

west

Aug. 10

ίσως

[ísos]

maybe

Aug. 11

καθαρός

[katharós]

clean

Aug. 12

μαθαίνω

[mathéno]

to learn

Aug. 13

τραπέζι

[trapézi] (neuter)

table

Aug. 14

γάντι

[gánti] (neuter)

glove

Aug. 15

καρότο

[karóto] (neuter)

carrot

Aug. 16

μπαταρία

[bataría] (feminine)

battery

Aug. 17

εκκλησία

[eklisía] (feminine)

church

Aug. 18

γάτα

[gáta] (feminine)

cat

Aug. 19

βαρετός

[varetós]

boring

Aug. 20

τσάι

[tsái] (neuter)

tea

Aug. 21

παιχνίδι

[pekhnídhi] (neuter)

game

Aug. 22

γυναίκα

[yinéka] (feminine)

woman

Aug. 23

φιλώ

[filó]

to kiss

Aug. 24

μπανάνα

[banána] (feminine)

banana

Aug. 25

δάσκαλος

[dháskalos] (masculine)

teacher

Aug. 26

στρατιώτης

[stratiótis] (masculine)

soldier

Aug. 27

έξυπνος

[éksipnos]

intelligent

Aug. 28

σακούλα

[sakúla] (feminine)

bag

Aug. 29

ηχηρός

[ikhirós]

loud

Aug. 30

δέντρο

[dhéntro] (neuter)

tree

Aug. 31

κλαίω

[kléo]

to cry

Sep. 1

γρήγορος

[grígoros]

fast

Sep. 2

αριστερός

[aristerós]

left

Sep. 3

λουλούδι

[lulúdhi] (neuter)

flower

Sep. 4

βρίσκω

[vrísko]

to find

Sep. 5

ημέρα

[iméra] (feminine)

day

Sep. 6

καρέκλα

[karékla] (feminine)

chair

Sep. 7

πρωί

[proí] (neuter)

morning

Sep. 8

φεγγάρι

[fengári] (neuter)

moon

Sep. 9

αρχίζω

[arkhízo]

to begin

Sep. 10

κεράσι

[kerási] (neuter)

cherry

Sep. 11

ποτέ

[poté]

never

Sep. 12

σπουδαίος

[spudhéos]

important

Sep. 13

λέξη

[léksi] (feminine)

word

Sep. 14

φρύδι

[frídhi] (neuter)

eyebrow

Sep. 15

θεία

[thía] (feminine)

aunt

Sep. 16

κλειδί

[klidhí] (neuter)

key

Sep. 17

μαγαζί

[magazí] (neuter)

store (shop)

Sep. 18

φως

[fos] (neuter)

light (e.g. from the sun)

Sep. 19

δεξιός

[dheksiós]

right (side)

Sep. 20

πορτοφόλι

[portofóli] (neuter)

wallet

Sep. 21

αγόρι

[agóri] (neuter)

boy

Sep. 22

ισχυρός

[iskhirós]

strong

Sep. 23

γραφείο

[grafío] (neuter)

office

Sep. 24

δόντι

[dhónti] (neuter)

tooth

Sep. 25

φωνή

[foní] (feminine)

voice

Sep. 26

όνειρο

[óniro] (neuter)

dream

Sep. 27

βροχή

[vrokhí] (feminine)

rain

Sep. 28

απλός

[aplós]

easy

Sep. 29

ώρα

[óra] (feminine)

hour

Sep. 30

ρολόι

[rolí] (neuter)

clock

Oct. 1

ιστορία

[istoría] (feminine)

story

Oct. 2

story

[ageládha] (feminine)

cow

Oct. 3

ψωμί

[psomí] (neuter)

bread

Oct. 4

θείος

[thíos] (masculine)

uncle

Oct. 5

αύριο

[ávrio]

tomorrow

Oct. 6

άθλημα

[áthlima] (neuter)

sport

Oct. 7

αγαπώ

[agapó]

to love

Oct. 8

αδελφή

[adhelfí] (feminine)

sister

Oct. 9

πυκνός

[piknós]

thick

Oct. 10

παλτό

[paltó] (neuter)

coat

Oct. 11

σπρώχνω

[sprókhno]

to push

Oct. 12

κλείνω

[klíno]

to close

Oct. 13

καπέλο

[kapélo] (neuter)

hat

Oct. 14

μυρίζω

[mirízo]

to smell

Oct. 15

ιδρώτας

[idhrótas] (masculine)

sweat

Oct. 16

φίλος

[fílos] (masculine)

friend

Oct. 17

πόλη

[póli] (feminine)

city

Oct. 18

γιαγιά

[yiayiá] (feminine)

grandmother

Oct. 19

τέχνη

[tékhni] (feminine)

art

Oct. 20

κολυμπώ

[kolimpó]

to swim

Oct. 21

μικρός

[mikrós]

small

Oct. 22

πόσο

[póso]

how

Oct. 23

μάτι

[máti] (neuter)

eye

Oct. 24

ακούω

[akúo]

to listen

Oct. 25

εφημερίδα

[efimerídha] (feminine)

newspaper

Oct. 26

χρήματα

[khrímata] (neuter)

money

Oct. 27

τσέπη

[tsépi] (feminine)

pocket

Oct. 28

άνδρας

[ándhras] (masculine)

man

Oct. 29

μουσική

[musikí] (feminine)

music

Oct. 30

Γη

[yi] (feminine)

Earth

Oct. 31

μεγάλος

[megálos]

big

Nov. 1

φθινόπωρο

[fthinóporo] (neuter)

autumn

Nov. 2

θυμάμαι

[thimáme]

to remember

Nov. 3

φαγητό

[fayitó] (neuter)

dinner

Nov. 4

παγωτό

[pagotó] (neuter)

ice cream

Nov. 5

όπου

[ópu]

where

Nov. 6

χάρτης

[khártis] (masculine)

map

Nov. 7

φωτιά

[fotiá] (feminine)

fire

Nov. 8

ενδιαφέρων

[endhiaféron]

interesting

Nov. 9

κρύος

[kríos]

cold

Nov. 10

στενός

[stenós]

narrow

Nov. 11

μήνας

[mínas] (masculine)

month

Nov. 12

τάξη

[táksi] (feminine)

class

Nov. 13

κανένας

[kanénas]

nobody

Nov. 14

νέος

[néos]

new

Nov. 15

μήλο

[mílo] (neuter)

apple

Nov. 16

σπουδαστής

[spudhastís] (masculine)

student

Nov. 17

χέρι

[khéri] (neuter)

hand, arm

Nov. 18

ξεχνώ

[ksekhnó]

to forget

Nov. 19

βάρκα

[várka] (feminine)

boat

Nov. 20

σάντουιτς

[sánduits] (neuter)

sandwich

Nov. 21

κίτρινος

[kítrinos]

yellow

Nov. 22

σκοτώνω

[skotóno]

to kill

Nov. 23

κάθομαι

[káthome]

to sit

Nov. 24

ευχαριστημένος

[efkharistiménos]

happy

Nov. 25

επιστήμη

[epistími] (feminine)

science

Nov. 26

κόκκινος

[kókinos]

red

Nov. 27

βιβλίο

[vivlío] (neuter)

book

Nov. 28

ρόδα

[ródha] (feminine)

wheel

Nov. 29

κεφάλι

[kefáli] (neuter)

head

Nov. 30

τρένο

[tréno] (neuter)

train

Dec. 1

πατάτα

[patáta] (feminine)

potato

Dec. 2

βούτυρο

[vútiro] (neuter)

butter

Dec. 3

παρκάρω

[parkáro]

to park (a car)

Dec. 4

λάδι

[ládhi] (neuter)

oil (cooking)

Dec. 5

ψηλός

[psilós]

tall

Dec. 6

γεύμα

[yévma] (neuter)

lunch

Dec. 7

τυρί

[tirí] (neuter)

cheese

Dec. 8

μπολ

[bol] (neuter)

bowl

Dec. 9

δουλεύω

[dhulévo]

to work

Dec. 10

δέρμα

[dhérma] (neuter)

skin

Dec. 11

χτυπώ

[khtipó]

to hit

Dec. 12

φόρεμα

[fórema] (neuter)

dress

Dec. 13

τραγουδώ

[tragudhó]

to sing

Dec. 14

μαγειρεύω

[magirévo]

to cook

Dec. 15

διαφορετικός

[dhiaforetikós]

different

Dec. 16

χθες

[khthes]

yesterday

Dec. 17

τρίχα

[tríkha] (feminine)

hair

Dec. 18

άσπρος

[áspros]

white

Dec. 19

κοιμάμαι

[kimáme]

to sleep

Dec. 20

σπίτι

[spíti] (neuter)

house

Dec. 21

γιος

[yios] (masculine)

son

Dec. 22

ηττώμαι

[itóme]

to lose (game)

Dec. 23

αυτοκίνητο

[aftokínito] (neuter)

car

Dec. 24

ευρύς

[evrís]

wide

Dec. 25

αέρας

[aéras] (masculine)

air

Dec. 26

αργός

[argós] (masculine)

slow

Dec. 27

ποδήλατο

[podhílato] (neuter)

bicycle

Dec. 28

βρώμικος

[vrómikos]

dirty

Dec. 29

φλιτζάνι

[flitzáni] (neuter)

cup

Dec. 30

δάχτυλο

[dhákhtilo] (masculine)

finger

Dec. 31

φτωχός

[ftokhós]

poor